A LIFE WORTH LIVING

By E. L. Warner

AN AUTHOR'S NOTE

The book that you are holding in your hands has been a project I've been working on for almost 15 years now. It has changed me in ways that cannot be described in words.

It is because of these changes that the tones, the time periods, and the lifestyles among each poem can change suddenly. Where there is improper grammar or "street slang", it has been left with intention to provide the impact and context of a given moment.

Each of these poems by themselves is just a glimpse into a small moment in time, and as a whole shows my journey from the classroom, to the train yards, to the streets, and back home again.

I have literally bled for some of these poems, and I wish it were a longer book and that I had more to offer you. However, if this book were any longer, then I fear that I wouldn't be here today.

I hope you enjoy this journey dear reader. I know I have.

Sincerely,
Eric L. Warner

Contents

COLUMBUS TO PHILLY

One.
Two.
Three.
Four.
I count the divider lines as they disappear under the truck.
The hood of our big rig eating them up like some,
insatiable beast.
"You and me" he says, "We're the last real cowboys."
He's right.
We're the last real vestige of the American West.
The thousand dead bugs and a cracked windshield tell the
stories of our cannonball runs.
Littered floors and bloodshot eyes have replaced our
calendars.
Local bartenders have replaced our therapists.
And the 8-track gives us hope with a steady beat.

"Fuck John Wayne!" he screams as he snorts a line and blows
past the weigh station.
This has been going on for three hours now, and I'm strangely
comfortable.

SANTA FE

Where God's colors renew the horizon's edge,
Salvation Soldiers aren't to be found.

While prairie dogs find themselves squatters on their own
land, upper crust artists show us where the day-old bread is.
This is a good place to clear your head, if there ever was one.
Where dusty markets, lead down dusty roads, that leads right
into the middle of where I want to be.

Free and Alone, on the side of a mountain, where the sun
don't apologize to me, and I don't have to explain myself to
anyone else.

Some go ahead and call this God's country.
I call this place New Mexico.

NORTH PHILLY BUS STOP CONVERSATIONS

Bus stop dreads stop me in my tracks because I'm too white to
be coming around here.
My clothes are too dirty and my smile's too honest.
I live a life of privilege that has nothing to do with the color
of my skin or the "insufficient funds" in my bank account.
Idle time is the devil's plaything they say,
But the devil has always sent his own to take care of me.
So, we just keep on walking, not to be judged by the race-
based politics, of those who have no recognized power over
us.

BOURBON STREET THIEVES

Perched under the Cat's Meow,
a nude lady flashes above my head.
With my hand on a smiley, and my eyes across the street,
I focus.
These streets are full of victims,
and she's not going to be one tonight.
Hurricane smiles squat next to me, and we're being eye-balled
from across the street.

It's time to go home.

PRIVATE STOCK CONVERSATIONS

My friend and I saw Val Kilmer make a meth deal last night,
and her nose started to itch.

We both used to ride the rails, but on completely different
lines.

Mine took me to new states.
Hers took her to a different state of mind.

I asked her to come with me once, in so many words.
Before I could ask her, "why not?" she asked the same of me.

I told her I was scared.
She said, "Me Too".

THOUGHTS ON AMERICA

A roar broke the silent dissidence of head shaking in a
conversation about America that I was in. This voice railed
against the country; whose pride ran deep in her blood.
And with this voice, I agree.

But it did cause concern when she lumped the red, the white,
the black and the blue in with the rusty freighters and rolling
hills that I've come to love.

And the concern brought forth lessons from my own teaching.
Stories of 15th century frontiersman tramping around the
"great wilderness", with nought even a flag to their name, for
they had rejected even that.

And memories of bloodline relatives that fought for the type
of independence that the declaration wasn't offering.
An independence from having unknown men, armed with
bibles, translated to the 19th power, telling them what's
"right" and "just".

Now here we are today, lying in a grave that is no longer
fresh whose tombstone reads: Democracy. All because we
have not yet understood that a flag is not a country, but rather
a symbol of control.

And a country!
Now there lies something to love.

And it's easiest to love in the labored breathing of a mountain top view, or in a toast from the top of a water tower overlooking the Mississippi.

It can be seen in the wave of a conductor as he pulls out of the yard. Or heard in the hissing of his wheels, when you have the moment of realization that, "Yes! Those trains are actually going somewhere!"

It can be grasped in the handshake of a homeless man, who is not unlike your forefathers. A castaway, tramping about the great wilderness with not even a flag or a prayer, but two hands that are ready to work for change.

FAIRY TALE SIDEWALKS

Goldilocks stopped on red.
I was waiting for green.
Blue eyes met for a moment,
When she saw me for what I was.
A rabbit in wolf's fur.
A drifter with a college education.

My eyes were not so honest.
And she passed by,
With a smile and a wave.

I might have been the luckiest man on campus that day.
I may have been the last.

FOR LINDSEY

A black miniskirt and a shitty band shirt.
She's wearing the same thing as the last time I saw her in
Missoula.
And Chicago before that.
Two wandering souls with the same flight pattern.
No matter where I went, that's where I was.
And so was she.
Chicago, Illinois.
Brattleboro, Vermont.
A rooftop in Philadelphia.
A graveyard in Iowa.
She's another ghost on this highway.
She bums a smoke,
We share a kiss,
And she's gone.

$4.29 FOR A PEN??

"That's outrageous!" He said.
"You're a goddamn fool." I muttered.
That's pennies on the dream.
If you think that the four dollars
And 29 cents is for a piece of plastic with some ink and a
ballpoint, then you're probably just making a grocery list.
A pen is not for scribbling to do lists.
There is an app for that.

A pen is for unlocking dreams and opening windows.
It's for recording the nightmares and victories of a life worth
living.
If you don't have PTSD from one thing or another by 28, then
you aren't living right.

"You're a madman" he chuckled.
Maybe so.
But I think the price is worth it.

THOUGHT PROCESS #1

As the gusts blow in from the south, dirty bundles huddle on
the shoreline. And as they rest their flea-bitten heads, they
dream of a time before this. When they were thought above
stray dogs.

Their waking hours focus on today. They focus on the
rocking steel, as it clickety-clacks the past.
They focus on eating.
They focus on the sun.
Women are a luxury when you're stark, raving, mad.

Of course, they don't actually think about any of that.
No one ever thinks about their unconscious decisions.
They act upon it.

They act upon growling stomachs with fine point sharpies put
to dumpstered cardboard. They act upon the holes in their
jeans, following the sun like any right-minded bird.

They'll follow it all the way to paradise. Surrounded by pink
Taffeta dresses and protective boyfriends.

They don't need to ask for a dance. They already left these
girls. It was in another town, and they had different names.
But it was them.

The ones that not only lit up the room, but sent the message
that you were somebody.

The ones who swore you were "the one" before leaving with the one.

And that's okay.

Because maybe they never believed her anyways.
Maybe they never believed in "the one" let alone, "just one."

Regardless, that was in another time in another place.
It's time to get focused.
It's time to get moving.
Only 10 more hours til we're hungry again.

OBSERVATIONS FROM YOUR SCHOOL JANITOR

I'm sitting in a strange man's house reading, "*STRANGER IN A STRANGE LAND*", and resisting the idea that I am another on a strain of poor marginalized Americans.

I'm a night janitor at an elementary school that goes unnamed. The kids smile and run past without a second thought.

My boss doesn't ask questions for his own reasons, and I just want my story to be heard.

My girlfriend is curled up on the futon behind me, and I'm wondering how I got so lucky.

There's a Francisco De Goya nude hanging above this overtly post-modern desk, and I'm eating at the soup kitchen tomorrow.

I stay inside most days, wrapped in a blanket, not realizing until too late that it's actually warm, and that the AC is turned up way too high.

GAINESVILLE NIGHTS

Gypsy smiles with aching minds, put forty-ounce bottles to pursed lips, and we're still not drunk enough to have excuses in the morning.

Our lives have become the lyrics to a Tom Waits anthem.

Dusty Carhartts and broken knuckles beg the question: "What kind of collective living exists when nobodies home?"

My mind is racing like the CSX flyby out of Baldwin, and I'm tempted to jump in front of that motherfucker tonight, cause I'm too scared to change the world.

She walks up and hugs me, and I pray that it's more than the beer hugging me. "Another World is Possible" is painted behind us in strokes of motivation the others just don't have.

There was no dust kicking up behind me as I walked away.

There wasn't even a break in the conversation.

FOR A MISSISSIPPI PIRATE QUEEN

She hugged me, and I breathed in deep.
Better than any perfume or cologne in the world, I know that
smell.
It's the scent of a thousand lost boy summers, fighting pirates
and chasing shadows.
It's rust dust and rail yards and campfire smoke.
It's gypsy smiles and moldy locks and secrets whispered
through the trees.
It's waking up to gentle words from complete strangers we
connected with the night before.
It's the scent of broken lips and battered kisses the morning
after Sturgis.
It's the sun glistening off an oil stain on the highway.
It's the scent of river washed clothes and ticks and lice and
fleas and kids named after all those things.

It's a scent of secret love affairs, and sexual exploration and
anarchist propaganda.
It's the smell of the E.L.F. and the Crimethinc. Ex Workers
Collective. It's the smell of the Wobblies.

But mainly, it's a smell that reminds me that they are still out
there, lying in wait in the shadows of the broken fence in the
rail yard.
Arms willing to hold you and fight for you, and never let you
go.

UNTITLED #1

I went to a poetry reading with a poet.
Then I had dinner with a mass murderer.
This is the dark and beautiful conundrum that has become my
life.

There's a photo of me as a baby:
My dad holds me in his full military regalia.
My mother stands next to him in a sundress, with flowers in
her hair.
I am a mixture of this and other confusing unions.

I am a devil's advocate.
An anarchist with a criminal complex.
A poet who would debate the need to cut down trees with the
Lorax, just so I could get a piece of paper to write these
thoughts down on.

I'm not always dark and hard.
If I was, I wouldn't be writing this.
I wouldn't be performing this.
I would just be.

And I can't think of anything sadder than that.

FOR A DRUNK GIRL I MET TODAY.

As a reformed Anonymist, I'm not one to look down on
drunks.
But today at the bar, I looked up at one and saw a beautiful
disaster.
Long dreaded hippie girls have a soft spot in the corner of my
heart.
From the patchwork dresses, to the oxymorons of a vegan
heroin addict; I've loved many.

But it's sad to watch someone create themselves through
liquor.
To create a persona through drugs because that's
"counter cultural."
To create another line of bullshit about not wanting to be a
robot.
A message so timeless and repetitive that it's...

She was actually kind of personable.
The few times that day she could speak, she was even funny.
She carried herself with a grace that was quite remarkable for
someone who could barely stand.
But she was on the run.
From a halfway house.
From a boyfriend.
From a drug.
From herself.

There's no truly meeting someone who is already halfway out
the door, and already in the bag.

There was a desperation in her smile that I've seen before in
my own reflection.
I don't believe in God.
But if you do, say a prayer for her.
I believe it's worth it.

AN OLD FLAME BURNED

She opened the lost journal,
and it was blank inside except
for the cover inscription.
It said that somebody loved her, who no longer did.
She scribbled it out like a lost opportunity,
and began writing a new chapter.

AN ACTION WORD

Love is a verb.
An action so intense that it scalds the tongue and makes those
three words difficult to say.
With each broken heart, scar tissue builds up along the palet
making it even more difficult to say.
The taste buds start to singe and the words taste bitter.
Then a new love comes along.
And her kisses are the aloe that opens up the vowels and
consonants of the heart, and allow me to speak softly and
concisely, until I am able to sing.

SOMETHING TO ADMIRE

I've been off the road for about 8 years now, but I still find a
need to sit by rivers.
Maybe it's a hobo thing.
Rivers provide water for drinking and washing.
They provide fish for eating and white noise for sleeping.
They take care of all those who take the time to stop and
acknowledge them.
And yet, a river never stops for you.
She doesn't even slow down.
Trains and people and love affairs all slow down.
Rivers just keep moving downstream, and they don't look
back.

UNTITLED #2

A Friday night in silence.
My mind races a hundred miles an hour.
Solitary confinement is the most dangerous thing to me.
I will either use it to destroy my world, or yours.

I'm not good at sitting still.
I die with stagnation.
On these nights, I drink until I can sleep, or stay amped until I
collapse.
I don't know how to shut down.

That's the same thing that keeps me going on the good days.

ON THE JOB TRAINING

"What do you do all night?" She wanted to know.
I didn't understand the question.
"Can we watch Netflix or something?"

No, no, no my newfound friend, this is not the place to
Netflix and Chill.
I need to teach you these things now.
I need to teach you because I need to spend one-third of my
life with you.

After having vowed to never get married, never settle down,
never have kids or college degrees, never spend another night
in jail, never waste another night fretting over whether I
should've called that hand or returned that call.

After all this, I'm still stuck with you.
Confined to the quiet of an empty building.
I've seen the world, and world history unravel and unfold
inside these walls.

I've walked through the remains of Chernobyl, looking over
the charred ashes and the shadows, and out into the vast
empty parking lots that stretch for miles.

I've held Geiger Counters in my hands and monitored for
signs of life, and pondered on how I managed to be the last
one standing. Gawking awkwardly at my sickly arms, and
wondering why they aren't glowing green.

I've stalked ancient tribes through the recesses of my mind.
Truly, the only explorer of a people that never existed outside
my own head.

A people with a passion for knowledge that exceeds the
Incas. They gather outside the palaces of Kings and Popes, in
order to hear their poetry in the mornings.

They never take it seriously, or cast aspersions, or build idols.
They only come to listen, and then.... they dissipate. They
head to their jobs in the markets, or on the docks, or to the
book binderies in the center of the city, since reading and
literature is considered my people's greatest currency.
And on the outskirts of town, there is a quiet army waiting.

Sometimes the building catches fire, or the flood rains come
down, or the sky opens up into a bloody storm of biblical
proportions.

Sometimes there's a tear in whatever dimension it is that stops
us from being able to see the spirit world, and I stand up on
the roof and see hundreds of ghosts walking around. Proving
once and for all that the dead stay with us, even after they're
dead.

We can feel their smiles in the car seat next to us, and we can
feel their disappointment when we don't understand why it all
happened like this.

Sometimes I'm a hitman or a hacker, or a ghost myself.
I think about if I died here tragically and my soul was stuck in

this ill-fitting suit forever. Would I care? Or would I be
ethereal so it wouldn't even matter?

Would I wander the halls on a constant tour of the buildings?
Stuck in my rounds for eternity, I'd look out the windows to
the park across the street and know that I would never feel the
dirt between my toes again.

This is my idea of hell.

Would other people be able to see me?
Would other guards quit because of the ghost of the guard
who died?

Sometimes I'm a ghost hunter, here to clear out a building
over the long weekend, before the workers come back on
Tuesday morning.

Sometimes I've sat in executive offices making decisions that
affect life or death.

I've hired and fired people who were going to change the
world with a new therapy or a medicine that would change
the fates of millions.

I've interviewed people and yelled at people and told them
that the only way to truth is out that fucking window. And it
doesn't matter that we're on the sixth floor, you have to jump.
Everything that matters in this life is a leap of faith.
And they always do.

They saunter past my desk, and open the window, and stand on a chair and casually step out.

Some of them smile. Their eyes closed, just feeling the rush of the wind on their face. Some of them soar.

They spread their arms, which the sun sets ablaze and burns away the flesh to reveal their wings underneath. They fly into the sun, and I try to watch them to figure out how it was done so that I too can fly away.

But the sun is bright and before I can catch a glimpse, I blink. And it's gone.

1ST TIME FOR EVERYTHING
(For Michelle)

The beat pulses.
The rhythm shakes.
She never breaks eye-contact as she serpentines
around me on the dance floor.
I thank god for that.
Because even after four whiskeys
I can tell
I'm an awful dancer.

UNTITLED #3

A veritable caricature of Jeremiah Johnson, I strung out on
Truth years ago.
Sitting amongst August sidewalks which sweat like a bitch in
heat, I verbally assault passersby.

With a slurred battle cry of "I can out Merlot you any day!" I
fall to my knees, unsure of which direction is up.
I try not to think of words like vertigo, or...
Vertigo.

A honking car sounds life back into me, but the windows are
tinted so I can't tell if I have it coming or not.
I flip em' the bird just to be safe.

THOUGHTS ON POETRY

Poetry is a fickle thing to be in a relationship with.
It is a domineering lover who does not know the meaning of
"later", but needs it done "Now! Now! Now!"
As such, I have had to pull the car over on the side of an
interstate, hit the 4-ways, and hope for the best.
All because I needed to scratch out some thoughts on love,
because maybe I'm on to something.
Or I sit in my office, which is an uninsulated closet filled with
disheveled thoughts, and pornography that pre-dates my
existence.
It is because of this chill in the air that most of my writing is
done at the bar, and with it the worry that those drinks seep
into my work more than they should.
Yet still lady poetry stays, if only to heckle that all my
favorite writers were acknowledged posthumously

GOOD TO>GOOD FOR

We were good to each other,
We were not good for each other.

The red-headed gypsy in thrift store Gucci.
We shared the same exact starting point in life.
We were born at the same time, on the same date, under the
same sun, with the same red hair.
We both carry with us, a mischievous grin.
She danced off the stage and into my heart, and I keep her
there today.
We are good to each other.
We were not good for each other.
A fair-haired Feline, who was fairly forgetful to boot.
Not someone I will ever forget.
I chased her to the ends of the earth, and then chased her off.
As though on a walk with Robert Frost, A fork appeared in
the road.
She broke up with me, because I had already left.
We were very good to each other,
We were not good for each other.
A native skinned beauty, who stole my heart for the better
half of a decade.
Our hearts fled to each other, while our bodies ran away.
On freight trains, in pirate caves, and under bridges, the
winds carried her kisses to me.
She's just as crazy as I am.
We are very good to each other.
We are not good for each other.

And yet...I think of you all the time

A TEACHERS ADVICE

I told her I am somebody new this year.
Someone with a story to tell.
Someone with something to write about.

Last year, I was a drug addict.
The year before that, I was a drug dealer.
The year before that, I lost all my money gambling.
The year before that, I tried to be a gambler.
The year before that, my sister picked me up
  in front of a Greyhound Station.
I didn't have any shoes.
I was trying to be a hobo.
The year before that, I was trying to be an artist...
  Or an alcoholic.
Whichever one drinks more.
The year before that, I dropped out of college.
The year before that, I tried to be a college student.

That year!
The year I started writing.
The year my words started to flow.
The year I had a teacher's love support me
  to the point where I left school.
That year, I tried to be a writer.
But I didn't have anything to write about.

She said, "Go try new things."

"Go be somebody new."

"Go be someone with a story to tell.

She told me, "Go be someone with something to write about."

CAMPING IS THE GREATEST SCAM OF THE CENTURY.

Her online dating profile said she was "Outdoorsy".
She asked if I wanted to go camping.
I told her, "No, I'm done camping."
I spent enough years sleeping outside,
and even more sleeping in the dirt.
It wasn't all bad.

I got to sleep with the stars, and wake up with the sun.
Once I woke up in the middle of a circle of deer.
I opened my eyes and the fawn looked at me, and I smiled.
She nodded at me, I swear to god she did.
Then she nudged her little ones awake, and they went off to
find another spot so I could get ready for the day.

I've encountered ghosts along the rivers, and thieves among
their banks.
I've never successfully started a fire without the aid of
Gasoline, and it cost me the title of King of the Hobos one
year.
Even as a homeless guy, I was mediocre.
I'm good at some things though.
I have references, I told her.

The next day, she deleted me from her favorites list.

AN ODE TO SANTA DE MUERTE

You came to me 12 years ago as I was laying in a gutter.
You stuck out your hand and said your name was Joe.
Your hand was neither cold nor clammy, like they say.
It welcomed me, without a second glance.
You've been with me throughout the years, in many forms.
You come to me in my dreams, and conquer my nightmares.
You came to me outside a bar, and took my finger off the
trigger.
You came to me in Louisiana and whispered that "Everything
Will Be Okay".
Then you told me to "run".
And run I did.
I haven't been back since, yet you remain beside me.

You are the calm in my rage.
You are the glint in my blank stare.
You temper my anger and chart a course for my wrath.

I've asked you for what I wanted, but you only give me what I
need.
We both understand that if I want anything more, I have to
take it.
And when I make a plan, and that smile creases my face, I
know that's your smile.

I can feel you looking out from behind my eyes when the
cocaine hits.
I can taste you in my kisses when I bite.
We are one and the same being, but you know so much more
than I ever can.

I learned patience when you locked me up.
I learned temperance when you released me.
You taught me how to hit someone with a claw hammer, then
you taught me how to stop.
You taught me that you don't need safe words when you
understand each other.

You are always with me.
Your cloak kept me warm when I lived on the street.
Your hands give me strength, when they guide my own.
And yet, I can offer you nothing.

I can't offer you my life, because it's yours any day you want
it.
I can't offer you my soul, because it's been yours for over a
decade.
I can't offer you fear, because I find comfort in knowing you
will be there at the end.
I can only offer you loyalty.
And return it to my family in kind.

FALLEN KINGS (FOR DUSTIN HO)

We've been sitting on the edge of the top of the city, watching
buildings scrape the sky.
The view is nice, but the ledge gives way.
Our assassins are moving in with smiles my Brother, so be
careful who you hug.
It's been said that the only ones who know where the edge is
have already gone over, and I disagree.
Time slows down when it's running out, and we can both feel
the wind upon our faces.
There's nothing to get upset about Brother.
It's only castles burning.

A PYRRHIC VICTORY

A mother is still crying in Ferguson, Missouri tonight.
There's no media coverage though.
They are all in Charleston.
Tomorrow, they will be somewhere else.
Once the cameras get turned off, and the microphones put
away, the story doesn't end.
There is still a father crying in Ferguson, Missouri tonight.

There are children crying in Minneapolis tonight.
There are dozens of young kids walking the hallways of their
school, searching for a man that will never walk them again.
There are still tears in Minneapolis tonight.

There is smoke and tears in Charleston tonight.
There is rage and exposed indignities.
There is corruption, and a systemic violence that we all
pretended was over on July 2, 1964.
But tomorrow, the cameras will be gone, and there will still
be tears in Charleston.
With so many tears, it's amazing the entire establishment
hasn't just been washed away, by a salt water flood.

A SIXTH SENSE

I had a dream last night that I was asleep, and my phone
started ringing.
I answered, "Who is this?", and a Scorpion replied.
He said he wants a meeting, and that "if you want to come
along,
you have to come alone."
So I got dressed in the dark.
Black pants.
Black shirt.
Black gloves.
Black gun.
I sat down at an empty table in an empty apartment,
and stared into the Scorpion's empty eyes.
He said, "I've been watching you."
Then he repeated that, "if you want to come along,
then you have to come alone."
I told him I've been alone my entire life, and he smiled.
The Scorpion asked if I had a wife or kids, "because if you
do…"
"I know." I said, "If I want to come along, then I have to
come alone."

The scorpion told me that he had made many men incredibly
wealthy.
I reminded him that he's also made many men incredibly
dead.
The Scorpion smiled.
"Do I have time to consider the offer?" I asked.
"I would expect nothing less from you." replied the Scorpion.

Then I woke up, covered in sweat.
I went to the bathroom, and I vomited.
As I was doubled over, I could hear my phone ringing.
I cleaned myself up, and answered it.

The voice on the other end said,
"Come see me tonight. And come alone."

THE LINE

Have you ever seen the line?
The before and after line.
The one that separates the seconds after now, from the ones a
few seconds before.
The line between "I love" and "you"
The line between "let's not and say we did" and "let's do and
say we didn't."
The line between the 10lb. Hammer and the silence of the
shot you never hear.
The line between walking away and looking over your
shoulder.
The line between "im sorry" and the stillness that follows.
The line between "please come back" and the upturned
corners of a dying mouth.
the letters written but never posted
the train of thought that crashed into the clouds
the words in the bottle that traveled the sea
but sunk to the bottom before it could ever reach you.

These are the most important moments in our lives. Moments
so thin, and meaningful that we can't see them coming.

ONE NIGHT IN PARADISE

The door is sealed, but voices ring out.
Purple Hearts still point the way.

There's a pipe in the corner that we're too afraid to pick up,
and microscopic devils reside in these sheets.

The screaming upstairs is getting louder.
This won't be the first time I've tried to hurt her.

Dirty rigs with missing caps make up our mind.
The floor is the safest route here.

This is home though, and love resides here.

    It shows itself among smelly blankets huddled
together in the midday sun.
    It's in the way permission is asked before saliva trades
with water.
    It smiles from behind broken skin and bruised eyes,
then saunters away to go spare change a meal.

FOR A GIRL IN SEATTLE

I met her through her brother.
He was a self-proclaimed anarchist activist, but it was in her eyes
   That I saw freedom.
We drank under bridges.
We howled at the moon.
We screamed at the sun.

And then she was gone.
And years went by.

Then she was back.
Returned from Brussels.
Speaking a new kind of language in a new tongue.
Once again, her eyes spoke of adventure, and her tongue tasted of travel.
I felt new winds, devoured new poems, and experienced new thoughts
   in her kisses.
We tried to stay in touch, and we managed to for a few breaths.

And then, I was gone.
And years went by.

We met again a few months ago.

We're both different now.
It's been ten years.

We speak less now than we did before, but we say more.
We've both learned the art of poetry, and not everything has
to be coarse.

I can sit quietly in a car with her, and twirl my fingers
between hers, and she can hear everything I'm not saying.

I can lay in bed with her, listening to our bodies listen to each
other, and I can breathe again.

THIS IS A TRUE STORY

I gave a homeless man a quarter yesterday,
and he threw it in the wishing well.
I went into the store and bought him a sandwich.
I brought it out to the wishing well, and sat down next to him.
He stared into the copper and silver waters and said,
"Thanks, but that wasn't my wish."

ABOUT THE AUTHOR

Born and raised in the Twin Cities, Eric Warner finds himself back in Minnesota after many years spent all over the map. While attending college in Putney, Vermont he decided that good poetry can't be written in basement classrooms with no windows. This is his debut attempt at putting his words into the world.

To get in touch with Eric Earner, email
Ewarner0907@gmail.com